MATH Trailblazers®

A BALANCED MATHEMATICS PROGRAM INTEGRATING SCIENCE AND LANGUAGE ARTS

Student Guide

Book 1

THIRD EDITION

KENDALL/HUNT PUBLISHING COMPANY
4050 Westmark Drive   Dubuque, Iowa 52002

A TIMS® Curriculum
University of Illinois at Chicago

MATH TRAILBLAZERS®

Dedication

This book is dedicated to
the children and teachers who
let us see the magic in their classrooms
and to our families who wholeheartedly
supported us while we searched for
ways to make it happen.

The TIMS Project

The original edition was based on work supported by the National Science Foundation under grant No. MDR 9050226 and the University of Illinois at Chicago. Any opinions, findings, and conclusions or recommendations expressed in this publication are those of the authors and do not necessarily reflect the views of the granting agencies.

Acknowledgments

Teaching Integrated Mathematics and Science (TIMS) Project Directors

Philip Wagreich, Principal Investigator
Joan L. Bieler
Howard Goldberg (emeritus)
Catherine Randall Kelso

Principal Investigators

First Edition	Philip Wagreich Howard Goldberg

Directors

Third Edition	Joan L. Bieler
Second Edition	Catherine Randall Kelso

Senior Curriculum Developers

First Edition	Janet Simpson Beissinger	Carol Inzerillo
	Joan L. Bieler	Andy Isaacs
	Astrida Cirulis	Catherine Randall Kelso
	Marty Gartzman	Leona Peters
	Howard Goldberg	Philip Wagreich

Curriculum Developers

Third Edition	Janet Simpson Beissinger	Philip Wagreich
Second Edition	Lindy M. Chambers-Boucher	Jennifer Mundt Leimberer
	Elizabeth Colligan	Georganne E. Marsh
	Marty Gartzman	Leona Peters
	Carol Inzerillo	Philip Wagreich
	Catherine Randall Kelso	
First Edition	Janice C. Banasiak	Jenny Knight
	Lynne Beauprez	Sandy Niemiera
	Andy Carter	Janice Ozima
	Lindy M. Chambers-Boucher	Polly Tangora
	Kathryn Chval	Paul Trafton
	Diane Czerwinski	

Illustrator

	Kris Dresen

Editorial and Production Staff

Third Edition	Kathleen R. Anderson	Christina Clemons
	Lindy M. Chambers-Boucher	
Second Edition	Kathleen R. Anderson	Georganne E. Marsh
	Ai-Ai C. Cojuangco	Cosmina Menghes
	Andrada Costoiu	Anne Roby
	Erika Larson	
First Edition	Glenda L. Genio-Terrado	Sarah Nelson
	Mini Joseph	Biruté Petrauskas
	Lynelle Morgenthaler	

Acknowledgments

TIMS Professional Developers

	Barbara Crum	Cheryl Kneubuhler
	Catherine Ditto	Lisa Mackey
	Pamela Guyton	Linda Miceli

TIMS Director of Media Services

Henrique Cirne-Lima

TIMS Research Staff

	Stacy Brown	Catherine Ditto
	Reality Canty	Catherine Randall Kelso

TIMS Administrative Staff

	Eve Ali Boles	Enrique Puente
	Kathleen R. Anderson	Alice VanSlyke
	Nida Khan	

Research Consultant

First Edition — Andy Isaacs

Mathematics Education Consultant

First Edition — Paul Trafton

National Advisory Committee

First Edition

	Carl Berger	Mary Lindquist
	Tom Berger	Eugene Maier
	Hugh Burkhardt	Lourdes Monteagudo
	Donald Chambers	Elizabeth Phillips
	Naomi Fisher	Thomas Post
	Glenda Lappan	

TIMS Project Staff

Table of Contents

Additional student pages may be found in the *Adventure Book* or the *Unit Resource Guide*.

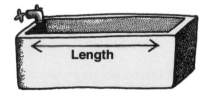

Length

Table of Contents

Additional student pages may be found in the *Adventure Book* or the *Unit Resource Guide*.

Dear Parents,

Math Trailblazers® is based on the ideas that mathematics is best learned through solving many different kinds of problems and that all children deserve a challenging mathematics curriculum. The program provides a careful balance of concepts and skills. Traditional arithmetic skills and procedures are covered through their repeated use in problems and through distributed practice. *Math Trailblazers,* however, offers much more. Students using this program will become proficient problem solvers, will know when and how to apply the mathematics they have learned, and will be able to clearly communicate their mathematical knowledge. Computation, measurement, geometry, data collection and analysis, estimation, graphing, patterns and relationships, mental arithmetic, and simple algebraic ideas are all an integral part of the curriculum. They will see connections between the mathematics learned in school and the mathematics used in everyday life. And, they will enjoy and value the work they do in mathematics.

The *Student Guide* is only one component of *Math Trailblazers.* Additional material and lessons are contained in the *Adventure Book* and in the teacher's *Unit Resource Guides.* If you have questions about the program, we encourage you to speak with your child's teacher.

This curriculum was built around national recommendations for improving mathematics instruction in American schools and the research that supported those recommendations. The first edition was extensively tested with thousands of children in dozens of classrooms over five years of development. In preparing the second and third editions, we have benefited from the comments and suggestions of hundreds of teachers and children who have used the curriculum. *Math Trailblazers* reflects our view of a complete and well-balanced mathematics program that will prepare children for the 21st century—a world in which mathematical skills will be important in most occupations and mathematical reasoning will be essential for acting as an informed citizen in a democratic society. We hope that you enjoy this exciting approach to learning mathematics and that you watch your child's mathematical abilities grow throughout the year.

Philip Wagreich

Philip Wagreich
Professor, Department of Mathematics, Statistics, and Computer Science
Director, Institute for Mathematics and Science Education
Teaching Integrated Mathematics and Science (TIMS) Project
University of Illinois at Chicago

Welcome to First Grade:
A Baseline Assessment Unit

	Student Guide	Adventure Book	Unit Resource Guide*
Lesson 1			
Look Around You		●	
Lesson 2			
We're Counting on You!	●		
Lesson 3			
The Train Game			
Lesson 4			
More or Less	●		

Unit Resource Guide pages are from the teacher materials.

Counting at the Toy Store

How Many Are There?

Count objects in the picture.

Object	Number Counted
clock	
horse	
teddy bear	
supercycle	
doll	

Name _____ Date _____

In My Home

Select and count objects such as clocks or shoes around your home. Write or draw each object in the table below. Record the number counted.

Object I Counted	Number

Name _____ Date _____

Measuring with Six Links

Your chain has six links. Use it to measure objects in the room. Is each object *more than, less than,* or *about the same* as six links? Complete the table.

Object	Circle One
	More than Less than About the same
	More than Less than About the same
	More than Less than About the same
	More than Less than About the same
	More than Less than About the same
	More than Less than About the same

Six Links at Home

Dear Family Member:

We are studying the ideas of *more than, less than,* and *about the same.* Please help your child complete the table below. Your child should write the name or draw a picture of five household objects in the left-hand column.

Thank you for your help.

Compare the length of each object with the six links on the right. Is the object's length *more than, less than,* or *about the same*? Circle your answer.

Object	Circle One
	More than Less than About the same
	More than Less than About the same
	More than Less than About the same
	More than Less than About the same
	More than Less than About the same

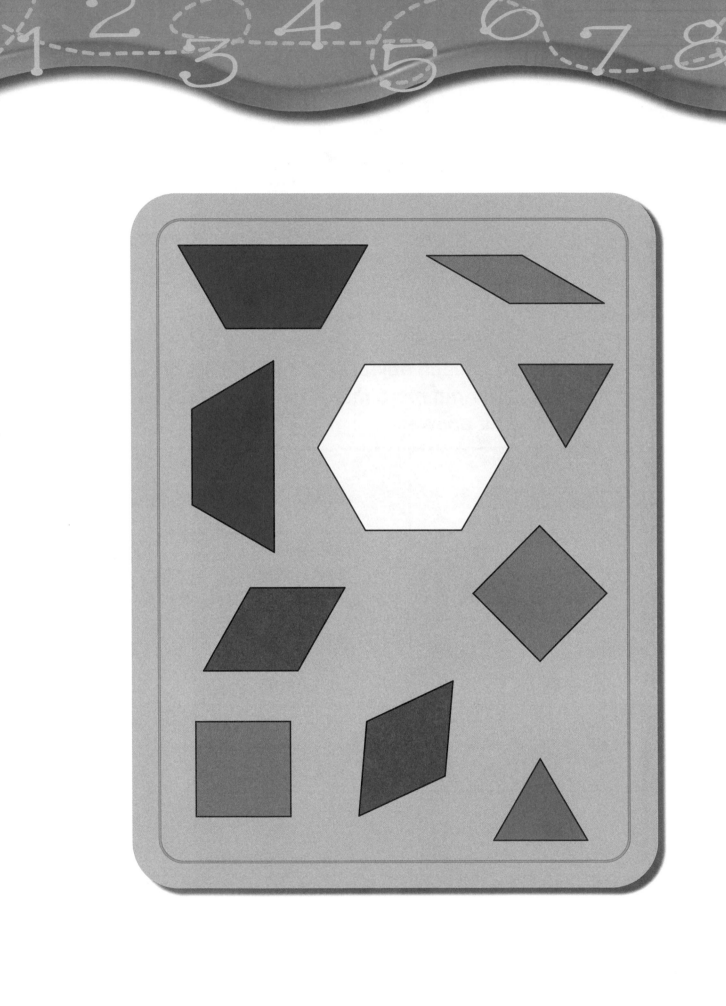

Unit 2

Exploring Shapes

	Student Guide	Adventure Book	Unit Resource Guide*
Lesson 1			
Shapes Around Us			
Lesson 2			
Describing Shapes	●		
Lesson 3			
Many Ways to Make a Hexagon	●		
Lesson 4			
How Many Does It Take?	●		
Lesson 5			
Mystery Figure			
Lesson 6			
Weather 1: Eye on the Sky	●		●

Unit Resource Guide pages are from the teacher materials.

11

Shapes in Nature

Nature is filled with shapes. Circle the shapes you see in the picture.

Describing Shapes

Name _____ Date _____

Nancy's Apartment and Yard

Homework

Dear Family Member:

Please help your child outline the shapes using the colors indicated below.
Encourage your child to use the names of the shapes.

Thank you.

Find the shapes. Outline triangles (▽, �￩) with red, circles (◯) with green, and rectangles (▭, ▯) with blue.

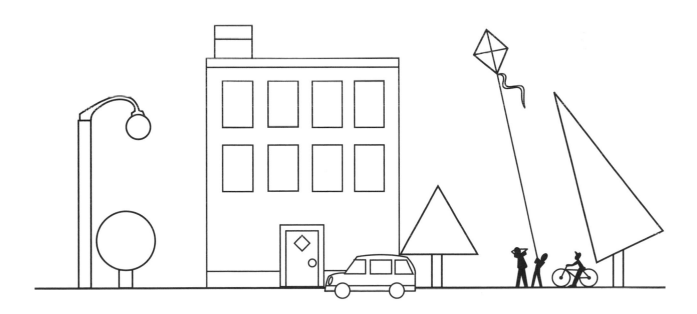

Describing Shapes

Alike and Different 1

One way these shapes are alike:

_____

One way these shapes are different:

_____

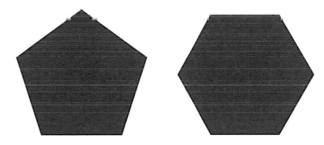

One way these shapes are alike:

_____

One way these shapes are different:

_____

Name _____   Date _____

Alike and Different 2

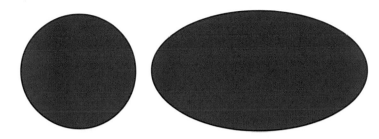

One way these shapes are alike:

_____

One way these shapes are different:

_____

One way these shapes are alike:

_____

One way these shapes are different:

_____

Name _____ Date _____

First Grade Times

First Graders Find Many Ways to Make a Hexagon

The Snake

Fill in the snake three different ways. Use pattern blocks.

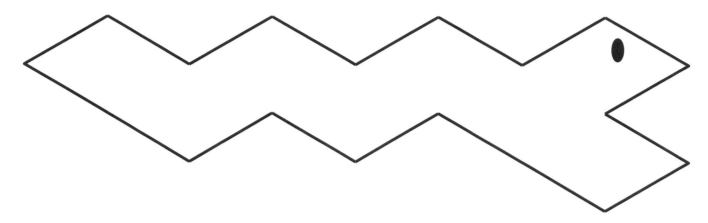

Write how many of each block you used.

Shape	First Way	Second Way	Third Way
⬡			
▼			
▲			
▮			
╱			
╱			
Total			

The Turtle

Fill in the turtle three different ways. Use pattern blocks.

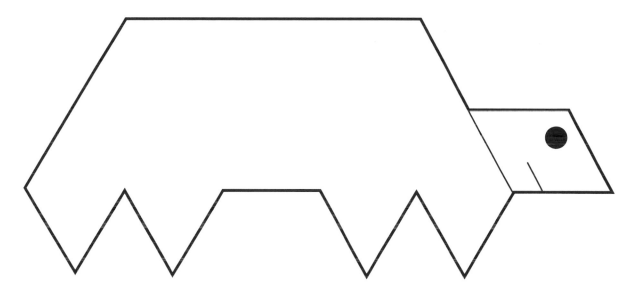

Write how many of each block you used.

Shape	First Way	Second Way	Third Way
⬡			
▽			
▲			
▪			
▱			
▱			
Total			

Name _____ Date _____

My Own Design

Make a design in the frame below. Use pattern blocks.

I made a design of _____

How many blocks did you use?

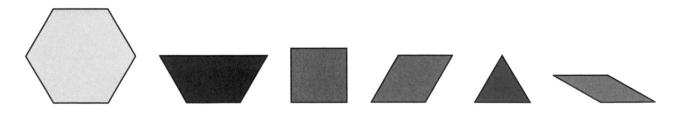

_____   _____   _____   _____   _____   _____

How Many Does It Take?

Name _____   Date _____

The Rocket

Fill in the rocket two different ways. Use pattern blocks. Then, write how many of each block you used.

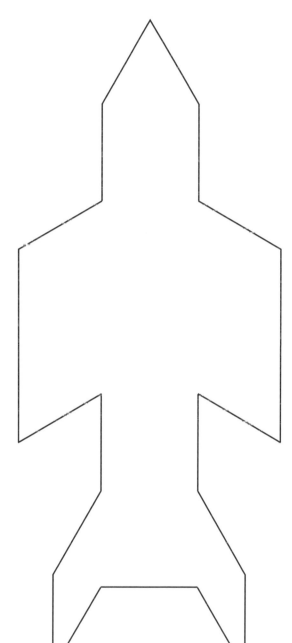

Shape	First Way	Second Way
⬡		
▽		
△		
▭		
▱		
▱		
Total		

Name _____ Date _____

Weather Calendar

Time of Day:

Month: _____ Year: _____

Sunday	Monday	Tuesday	Wednesday	Thursday	Friday	Saturday

Name _____ Date _____

Weather 1 Data Table

Study your *Weather Calendar*. Record the data in the table below.

| *T*
Type of
_____ | *N*
Number of _____ | |
	Tallies	Total

Weather 1 Graph

Make a graph of your data.

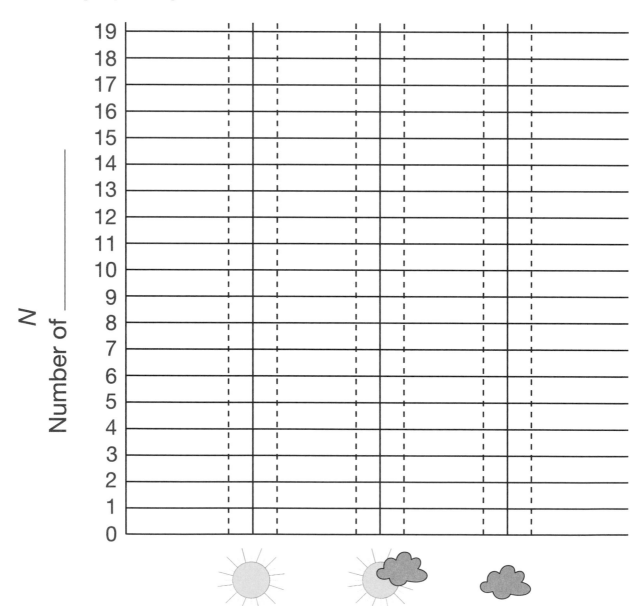

N

Number of _____

Type of _____

Name _____ Date _____

Thinking about the Weather

Answer the following questions. Use your data table and graph.

1. Which type of sky did you see *most* often?

    _____

2. Which type of sky did you see *least* often?

    _____

3. How many sunny *and* partly sunny skies were there in all?

    _____

4. **A.** Were there more cloudy skies or more sunny skies?

    _____

    B. How many more?

    _____

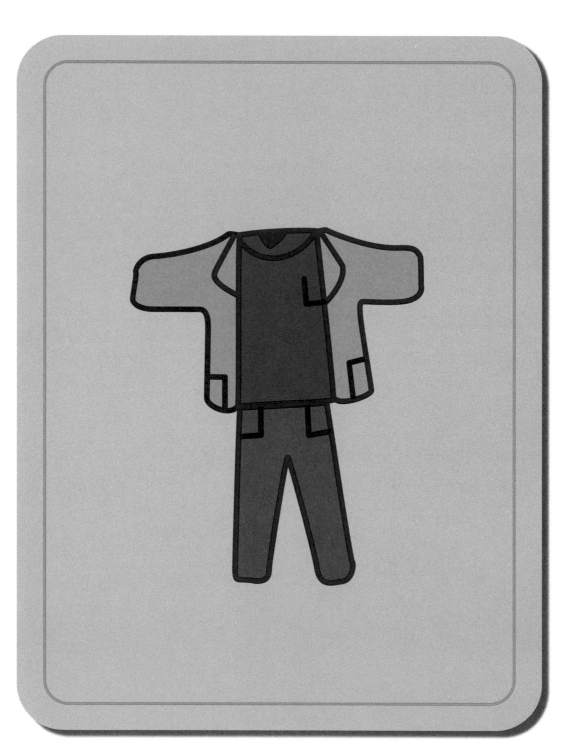

Pennies, Pockets, and Parts

	Student Guide	Adventure Book	Unit Resource Guide*
Lesson 1			
Favorite Colors	●		
Lesson 2			
Ten Frames	●		
Lesson 3			
Think and Spin	●		
Lesson 4			
Pockets Graph			
Lesson 5			
Pocket Parts	●		●
Lesson 6			
What's in That Pocket?	●		
Lesson 7			
Purchasing with Pennies	●		

Unit Resource Guide pages are from the teacher materials.

Name _____ Date _____

Kitchen Tools

Count and tally the objects in the table.

Objects	Tallies	Total

Name _____ Date _____

House Walk

Dear Family Member:

Please help your child count the objects listed in the table. As you go from room to room, have your child record a tally for each object he or she sees. After all of the rooms have been checked, have your child count the tallies and record the total.

Thank you for your cooperation.

Record a tally for each object in your home. Then, count the tallies and record the total.

Object	Tallies	Total
Lamp		
Chair		
Table		
Clock		
Window		

Name _____ Date _____

Ten Frames

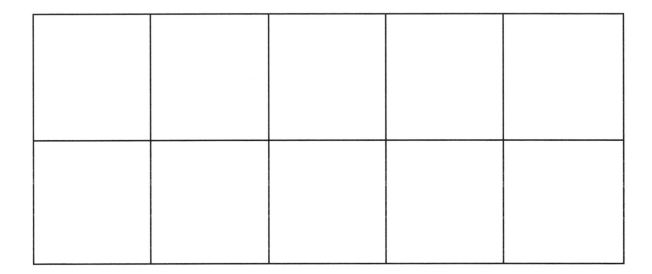

What's My Number?

How many counters are in each ten frame? Write the number on the line.

1.

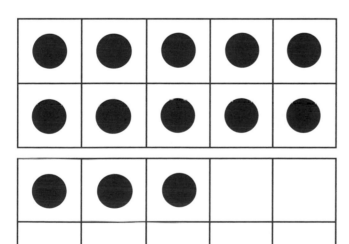

_____

2.

_____

3.

_____

4.

_____

Number Sentences

Write a number sentence for each question.

1.

□ + □ = □

2.

□ + □ = □

3.

□ + □ = □

4.

□ + □ = □

What's My Sentence?

Write a number sentence for each question.

1.

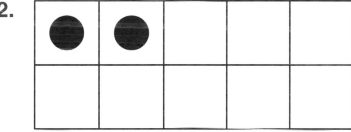

☐ + ☐ = ☐

2.

☐ + ☐ = ☐

3.

☐ + ☐ = ☐

4.

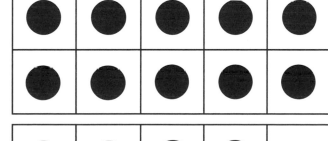

☐ + ☐ = ☐

Think and Spin

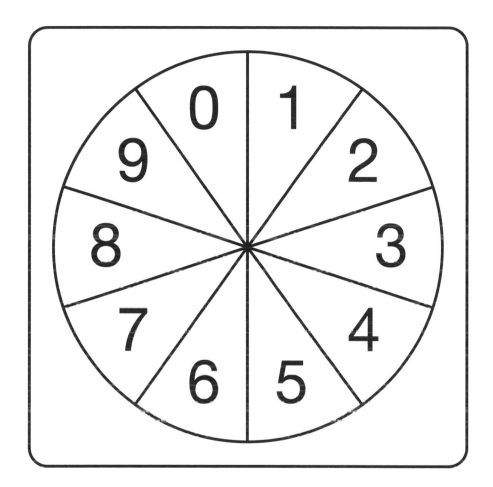

Name _____ Date _____

Ten Frame Recording Sheet

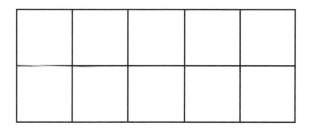

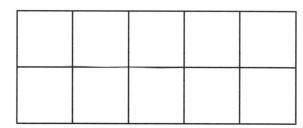

_____   _____

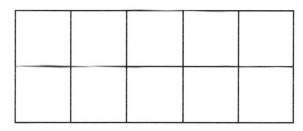

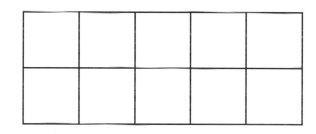

_____   _____

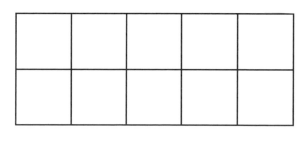

_____

Wearing Pockets

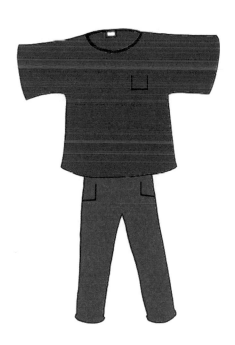

Homework

Dear Family Member:

Tomorrow your child will gather data and make a bar graph. We will count the number of pockets on each student's clothing. Please help your child select clothing that has pockets on the pants, skirt, or shirt.

Thank you for your help.

Shirt and Pants Pockets

Record the number of shirt pockets, pants pockets, and total pockets. Then, write a number sentence.

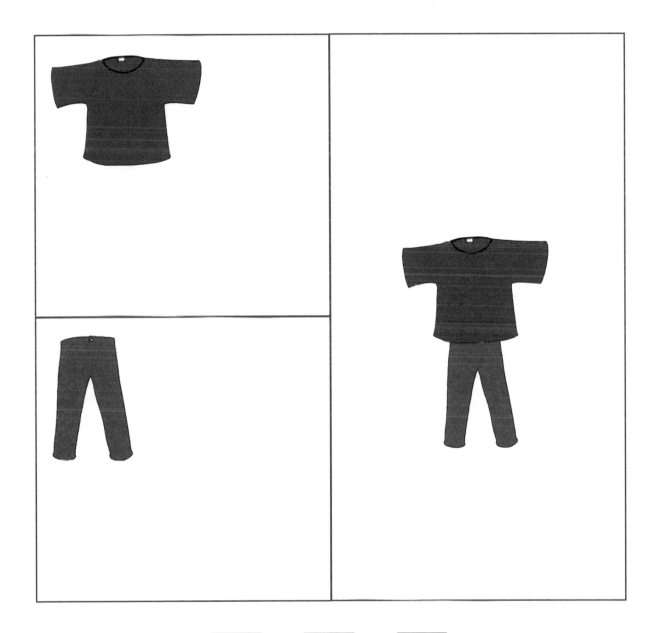

☐ + ☐ = ☐

Name _____ Date _____

Pocket Parts 1

Find the total number of pockets for each. Then, write a number sentence for each.

1.

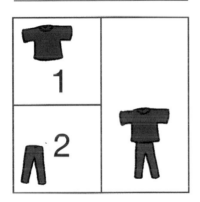

$$1 + 4 = 5$$

2.

_____

3.

_____

4.

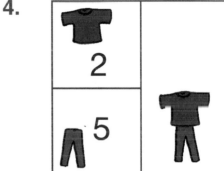

_____

5.

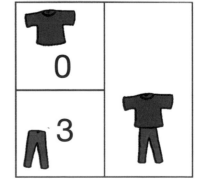

_____

6.

_____

Name _____ Date _____

Pocket Parts 2

Find the total number of pockets for each. Then, write a number sentence for each.

1.

$$4 + 4 =$$

2.

_____

3.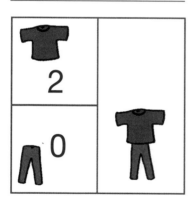

_____

4.

_____

5.

_____

6.

_____

Name _____   Date _____

How Many Pockets?

Find the total number of pockets for each. Then, write a number sentence for each.

1.

$$\underline{\ 2 + 2 + 4 = 8 \ }$$

2.
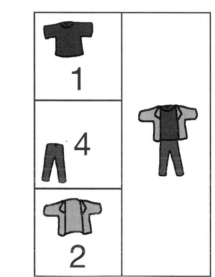

_____

3.

_____

4.

_____

Hidden Pockets

Find the number of pants pockets for each student. Then, write a number sentence for each.

1.
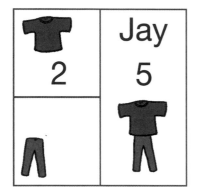
Jay

$2 + 3 = 5$

2.
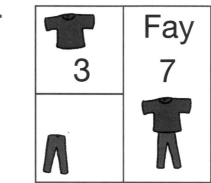
Fay

_____

3.
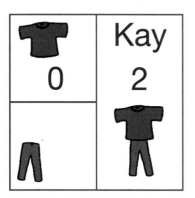
Kay

_____

4.
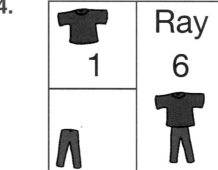
Ray

_____

5.

May

_____

6.
Shay

_____

Pockets

Find the missing number of pockets for each problem. Then, write a number sentence for each.

1.

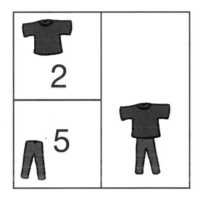

_____

2.

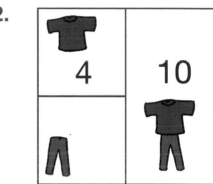

_____

3.

_____

4.

_____

Two Pockets Work Mat

Place your pennies on the pockets. Record on the data table the different ways you can arrange them.

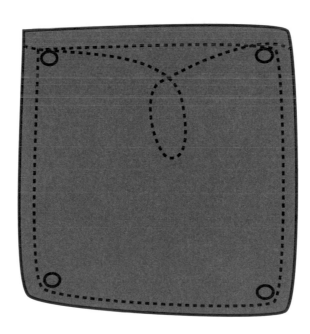

Two Pockets Data Table

How many ways can you arrange ten pennies in two pockets? Record as many ways as you can. Then, write a number sentence for each one.

		Total Pennies	Number Sentence
6	4	10	6 + 4 = 10

Three Pockets Work Mat

Place your pennies on the pockets. Record on the data table different ways you can arrange them.

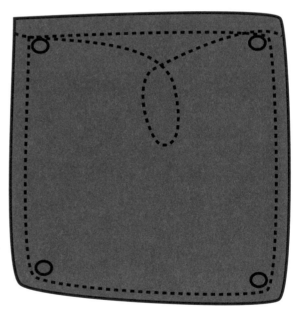

Three Pockets Data Table

How many ways can you arrange ten pennies in three pockets? Record as many ways as you can. Then, write a number sentence for each one.

			Total Pennies	Number Sentence
1	2	7	10	1 + 2 + 7 = 10

Eight Pennies Data Table

Homework

Dear Family Member:

Your child will need eight pennies for this assignment. He or she should divide the pennies in different combinations between two pockets. The total should equal eight for each problem. Please help your child complete the data table.

Thank you.

How many ways can you arrange eight pennies in two pockets? Record as many ways as you can. Then, write a number sentence for each one.

		Total Pennies	Number Sentence
0	8	8	0 + 8 = 8

Nine Pennies Data Table

How many ways can you arrange nine pennies in two pockets? Record as many ways as you can. Then, write a number sentence for each one.

		Total Pennies	Number Sentence

What Would I Buy?

Homework

Dear Family Member:

Look at the items below with your child. Ask him or her to read the price for each item. Help your child with the reading of each question. Give your child pennies to help him or her decide which items to circle. To answer Question 2, your child could draw a picture or use a number sentence (for example, 5¢ + 3¢ = 8¢).

Thank you for your cooperation.

Look at the items below.

5¢   4¢   3¢   2¢

1. Circle the items you would buy if you had ten pennies. (If you want two of the same item, make two circles around it.)

2. How much would you pay for all the items you circled? Show how you found your answer.

   _____

3. Would you have any pennies left over? How many?

   _____

4. Make up a problem for other students to solve.

   _____

Unit 4

Adding to Solve Problems

	Student Guide	Adventure Book	Unit Resource Guide*
Lesson 1			
Exploring Even and Odd Numbers	●		
Lesson 2			
The Pet Shop	●		
Lesson 3			
Parts and Wholes	●		●
Lesson 4			
Counting On to Add	●		

Unit Resource Guide pages are from the teacher materials.

Even or Odd?

1. Write a number for each picture.

   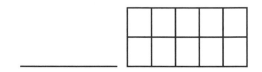

   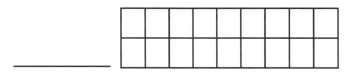

   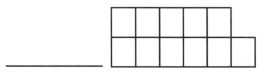

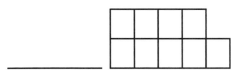   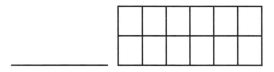

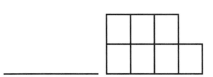   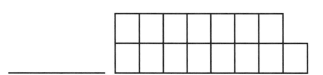

2. Circle the even numbers.

3. Look at the pictures above. Which numbers are odd?

_____

Name _____   Date _____

Is My Home Even or Odd?

Homework

Dear Family Member:

Your child is learning how to tell if a number of objects is even or odd. Help your child count the objects listed below. Record the numbers in the table. Encourage him or her to show the number of each object with pennies or other counters. Your child should pair up the counters. If there is one left over, the number is odd.

Thank you.

Example:

The number seven is odd because there is one left over.

A number such as six is even because there are no leftovers.

Object	Number of Objects in My Home	Even or Odd
Chairs		Even or Odd
Rugs		Even or Odd
Lamps		Even or Odd
Tables		Even or Odd
Shoes		Even or Odd
Spoons		Even or Odd

Animals in the Pet Shop

Pets at Home

Use a calculator to solve the following problems.

1. Sylvia's block has three kittens and five puppies. How many pets are on Sylvia's block? Press the keystrokes below to find out.

| 3 | + | 5 | = |

2. For each problem, fill in the missing keystroke boxes. Then, find the answer.

   A. Marcus's block has 5 dogs and 11 cats. How many dogs and cats do they have?

| 5 | + | | = |

   B. Tom's family has 2 pets. There are 16 other pets in Tom's building. How many pets are in the building?

| | + | | = |

   C. Marsha counted 12 dogs and 13 cats on her block. How many pets are there in all?

| | | | |

   D. Samantha has two turtles, five frogs, and six lizards as pets. How many pets does Samantha have?

| | | | | | |

Animal Addition Stories

Dear Family Member:

Your child is writing and developing addition stories in the classroom. Help him or her write addition stories about animals. Include number sentences. Encourage your child to illustrate the stories.

Thank you for your help.

Example:

Janice has two dogs and three cats in her home. She has five pets in all. (2 + 3 = 5)

Write three addition stories about animals. Draw a picture about your stories.

Addition Story 1:

_____

_____

_____

_____

_____

Picture:

Name _____ Date _____

Addition Story 2:

_____

_____

_____

_____

Picture:

Addition Story 3:

_____

_____

_____

_____

Picture:

The Pet Shop

Name _____ Date _____

Parts and Wholes

I am showing different ways to make _____.

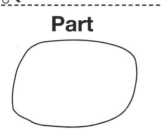 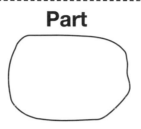

Part   **Part**

_____ + _____ = _____

Part   **Part**

_____ = _____ + _____

Part   **Part**   **Part**

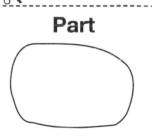 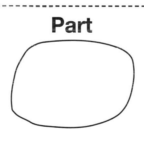 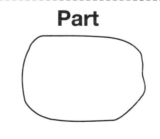

_____ + _____ + _____ = _____

Part   **Part**   **Part**

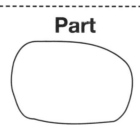 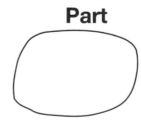 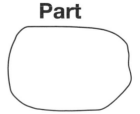

_____ = _____ + _____ + _____

Name _____ Date _____

It's in the Mail

Use the calendar to help you find the date the mail arrived.

Sunday	Monday	Tuesday	Wednesday	Thursday	Friday	Saturday
						1
2	3	4	5	6	7	8
9	10	11	12	13	14	15
16	17	18	19	20	21	22
23	24	25	26	27	28	29
30	31					

Date Sent	Arrived	Number Sentence	Date Received
mailed 10	3 days later	_____	☐
mailed 13	2 days later	_____	☐
mailed 24	4 days later	_____	☐
mailed 30	1 day later	_____	☐
mailed 5	5 days later	_____	☐
mailed 17	3 days later	_____	☐
mailed 20	5 days later	_____	☐
mailed 14	4 days later	_____	☐

Name _____ Date _____

Happy Helpers Club

Homework

Dear Family Member:

In class, your child uses the counting-on strategy to solve problems. To do 11 + 3, for example, start by saying "11" and then count on, "12, 13, 14." Encourage your child to use counting on to solve the problems below.

Thank you.

How much money will each student have after receiving 3 more cents?

13¢ + 3¢ = _____   18¢ + 3¢ = _____   20¢ + 3¢ = _____

24¢ + 3¢ = _____   29¢ + 3¢ = _____   32¢ + 3¢ = _____

Coin Jar

Homework

Dear Family Member:

Make a coin jar. Stock a small jar with a few nickels and
20 to 30 pennies. Ask your child to remove a few coins from
the coin jar. Help your child name the coins and find their value.
Then, record the amount on the first purse. Repeat for each of the
other purses.

Thank you.

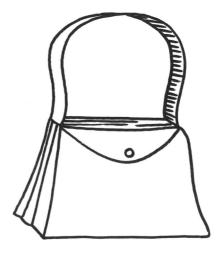

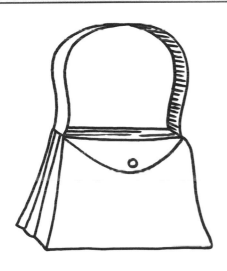

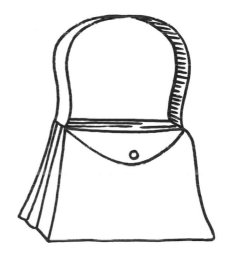

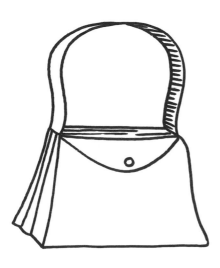

Grouping and Counting

	Student Guide	Adventure Book	Unit Resource Guide*
Lesson 1			
Skip Counting	●		
Lesson 2			
Counting by Fives and Tens	●		
Lesson 3			
Sharing Cookies	●		●
Lesson 4			
I've Got a Little List		●	
Lesson 5			
Colors	●		●

Unit Resource Guide pages are from the teacher materials.

Name _____   Date _____

Counting by Twos

Homework

Dear Family Member:

Your child is learning to skip count by twos. Discuss things that come in twos such as shoes and twins. Encourage your child to skip count by twos to complete this page.

Thank you.

A. Count the eyes by twos.

2, _____, _____   There are _____ eyes.

B. Count the bicycle wheels by twos.

2, _____, _____, _____, _____   There are _____ wheels.

C. Count the mittens by twos.

2, _____, _____, _____, _____, _____, _____

There are _____ mittens.

Things in Twos

Homework

Dear Family Member:

Your child is learning how to skip count by twos. Discuss things that come in groups of two such as wheels on a bicycle and ears. Have your child choose an object that comes in twos, draw several of them, and then count, in twos, the number he or she drew. Help your child complete the bottom of the page.

Thank you.

Find things that come in twos. Then, draw and count them.

I counted twos like this:

2, _____, _____, _____ , _____, _____, _____, _____, _____, _____, _____

What did you draw? _____

How many did you draw? _____

Name _____ Date _____

Ten Frames

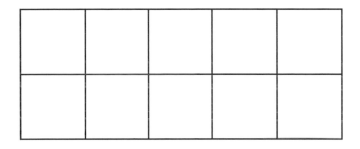

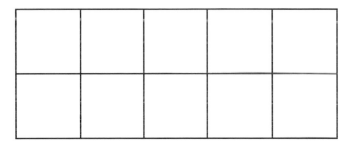

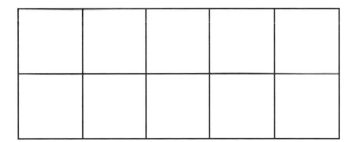

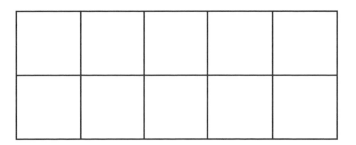

Fair Shares

Share cookies as shown in the table below.

The total number of cookies = _____

People	Fair Shares	Leftovers	Words
☺ ☺			Two groups of _____ and _____ left over
☺ ☺ ☺			Three groups of _____ and _____ left over
☺ ☺ ☺ ☺			Four groups of _____ and _____ left over
☺ ☺ ☺ ☺ ☺			Five groups of _____ and _____ left over
☺ ☺ ☺ ☺ ☺ ☺			Six groups of _____ and _____ left over

Packing Grandma's Cookies

Help Grandma pack her cookies. Arrange your counters in groups of ten. Draw one box for every group of ten. Then, draw the leftovers.

Work Slip 1	Number of Cookies	Boxes	Leftover Cookies

Work Slip 2	Number of Cookies	Boxes	Leftover Cookies

Cookie Factory

Homework

Dear Family Member:

Help your child group cookies in boxes of ten. Encourage him or her to draw the boxes and the leftover cookies. Your child may need counters such as beans to solve these problems.

Thank you for your help.

Count, group, and box the cookies. Record your answers below.

		Number of Cookies	Boxes	Leftover Cookies
A.	Work Slip	22		
B.	Work Slip	26		
C.	Work Slip	35		
D.	Work Slip	39		
E.	Work Slip	50		

Colors Picture

Draw a picture of the experiment.

Colors Data Table

Total number of pieces in my sample ——————————

Colors

C Color	P Number of Pieces

Colors Graph

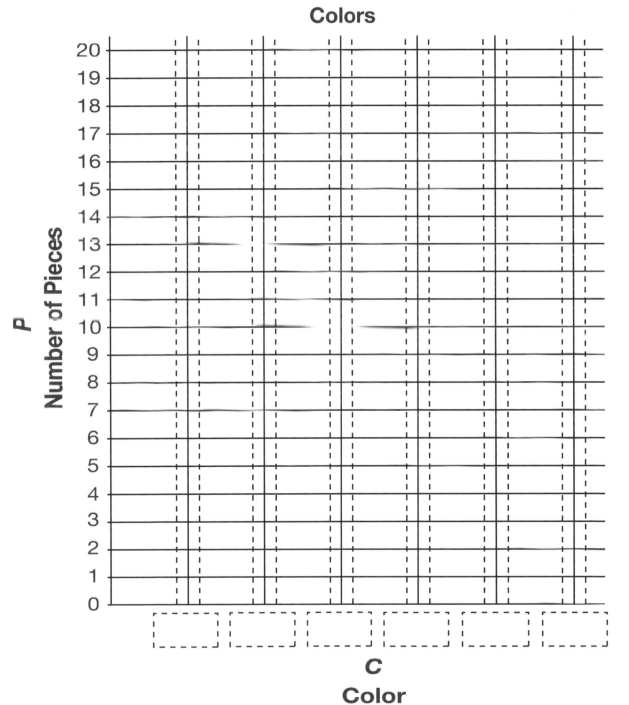

Colors

P
Number of Pieces

C
Color

Reading a Colors Graph

Mary's Class Graph

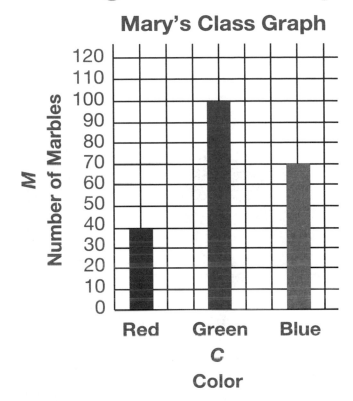

1. How many red marbles did Mary's class pull out altogether?

   _____

2. What color was most common? _____

3. The principal took a handful of marbles. Predict which color was most common in her handful.

   _____

4. Combine the blue and the red marbles Mary's class pulled out. Is this number more than the number of green ones?

   _____

Unit 6

Measurement: Length

	Student Guide	Adventure Book	Unit Resource Guide*
Lesson 1			
Linking Up	●		
Lesson 2			
Rolling Along with Links	●		
Lesson 3			
Betty Builds a Better Racer		●	
Lesson 4			
Using Unusual Units	●		
Lesson 5			
Delightful Dachshunds	●		
Lesson 6			
Give 'em an Inch	●		

Unit Resource Guide pages are from the teacher materials.

Measuring Our World

Here are some things in Maria's classroom. How do they compare with those things in your classroom? Measure to find out.

Maria's desk is 18 links tall.

1. My desk is _____ links tall.

Maria's desk is 24 links long.

2. My desk is _____ links long.

Maria measured the distance around her math book. The distance around an object is called the **perimeter.**

The perimeter of Maria's math book is 39 links.

3. The perimeter of my *Student Guide*

is _____ links.

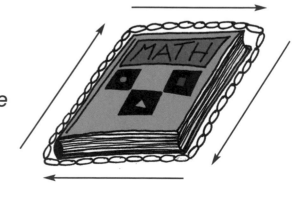

Name _____ Date _____

Measuring Ourselves

Julio's arm is 12 links long.

1. My arm is _____ links long.

Julio's foot is 5 links long.

2. My foot is _____ links long.

3. Use links to measure another part of your body. Draw a picture to show what you measure.

My _____ is _____ links long.

Rolling Along with Links

Draw a picture of the experiment setup. Include the parts of the experiment that must remain the same.

Name _____ Date _____

How far did each type of car roll? Record the distance in the data table below.

Rolling Along with Links

T Type of Car	D Distance Rolled (in links)

•

Make a bar graph of your data. Remember to fill in the proper units.

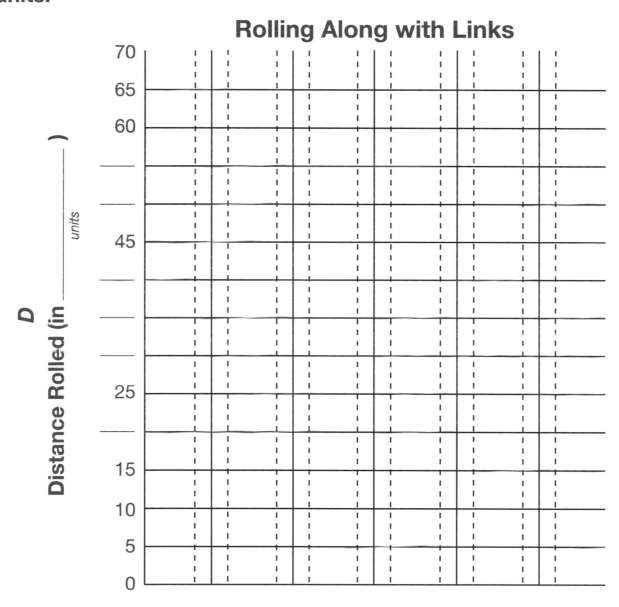

Rolling Along with Links

70
65
60

45

25

15
10
5
0

D
Distance Rolled (in _____)
units

T
Type of Car

Answer the questions below. Use your data table and graph.

1. Which car was the best roller? _____

2. How far did the best roller go? _____

3. Which car was the worst roller? _____

4. How far did the worst roller go? _____

5. How much farther did the best roller go than the worst roller? Discuss how you found your answer.

   _____

6. Susan's car rolled 20 links. David's car rolled 12 links farther than Susan's. How far did David's car roll?

   _____

7. Write a number sentence for your answer to Question 6.

   _____

8. Tom's car rolled 17 links. Rico's car rolled 20 links. How much farther did Rico's car roll?

   _____

9. Write a number sentence for your answer to Question 8.

   _____

Two Car Roll-off

Homework

Dear Family Member:

Your child completed a lab where he or she rolled cars down a ramp and used links to measure the length the cars traveled. Help your child count the links in the picture below and complete the questions.

Thank you.

Two cars rolled from two ramps. In the drawing below, you are seeing the tops of the cars from above.

1. How far did car A roll? _____

2. How far did car B roll? _____

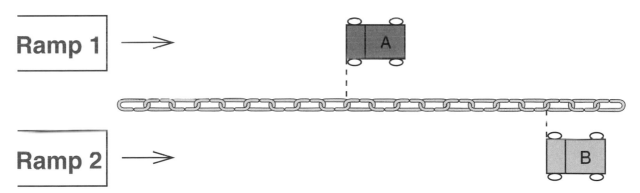

3. How much farther did car B roll than car A?

_____

4. Why might car B have rolled farther?

_____

_____

Name _____ Date _____

Brian's Class

Brian's class found the data shown in the graph below.

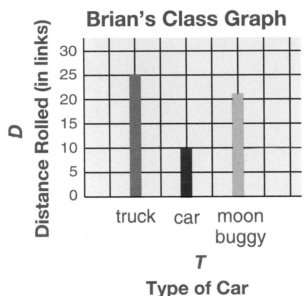

Brian's Class Graph

1. Which was the best roller?

   _____

2. Which was the worst roller?

   _____

3. How much farther did the truck travel than the car?

   _____

4. About how far did the moon buggy roll?

   _____

5. How much farther would the truck have to roll to reach a distance of 30 links?

   _____

Watch Your Step

Measure distances in your classroom. Use the length of your foot. Record your measurements in this table.

From	To	Number of

Unusual Units

Estimate how many of each unit you need to measure a bathtub.

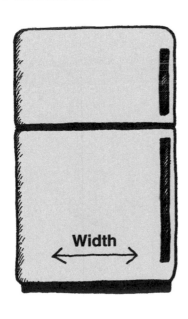

Length

Unit	Length of Tub
soap ▫	_____
toothbrush 🪥	____10____
washcloth ▨	_____
hand towel 🐟	_____

It takes 3 soda pop bottles to measure the width of a refrigerator. Match the rest of the numbers with their units of measure.

Width

Width of Refrigerator	Unit
____12____	• grape
____9____	2-liter soda pop
____3____	apple
____35____	MARGARINE margarine

Measuring at Home

Homework

Dear Family Member:

The boy in the picture is measuring a bed. He is using the edge of a paper towel as a unit. Help your child measure four things in your home using one object as the unit of measure. Some objects you might use as tools for measuring are a cooking utensil, a cereal box, a pencil, or a book.

Thank you.

Record your data in the table below.

Four Things Measured at Home

Things I Measured	Length Measured Using _____

Stepping Out with My Family

Homework

Dear Family Member:

Your child used footsteps to measure distances in the classroom. Encourage your child to measure straight distances in your home by counting steps as he or she walks "heel-to-toe." For example, your child might walk from the refrigerator to the kitchen table. Ask your child to write or draw pictures in the "From" and "To" columns to indicate the starting and stopping points. After your child measures and records the distances, ask him or her to predict the measurement if your footsteps were used. Check your child's prediction by measuring each distance using your footsteps. Ask your child to record your measurements.

Thank you.

Measure distances in your home. Then, record the data in the table below.

Distances in My Home

From	To	Number of My 👣	Number of Your 👣

Delightful Dachshunds

1. Which dog is longer? Make a prediction. Then, make link and cube chains to compare the lengths. Write the name of the dog in the box.

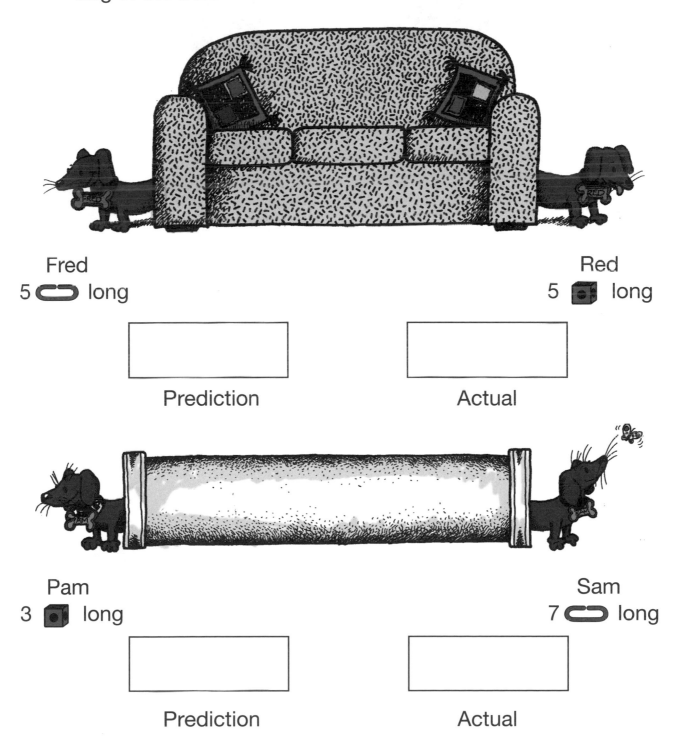

Fred

5 🔗 long

Red

5 🔲 long

| |
| |

Prediction

| |
| |

Actual

Pam

3 🔲 long

Sam

7 🔗 long

| |
| |

Prediction

| |
| |

Actual

Buddy	Buster
5 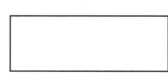 long	6 ▣ long

Prediction   Actual

2. Which length is longer? Make a prediction. Then, compare the lengths of the link and cube chains. Circle the longer one.

Prediction		Actual	
18 ⬭ long	25 ▣ long	18 ⬭ long	25 ▣ long
9 ⬭ long	8 ▣ long	9 ⬭ long	8 ▣ long
3 ⬭ long	7 ▣ long	3 ⬭ long	7 ▣ long
8 ⬭ long	12 ▣ long	8 ⬭ long	12 ▣ long

Comparing Links and Cubes

Predict the longer length. Make chains of links and trains of cubes. Then, circle the longer one.

	Prediction		**Actual**	

A.

Prediction: 9   13
Actual: 9   13

B.

Prediction: 20   20
Actual: 20   20

C.

Prediction: 13   23
Actual: 13   23

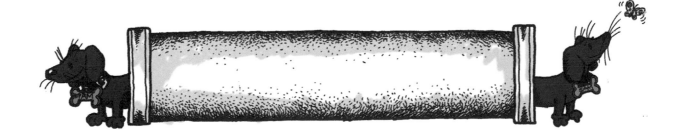

Could Be or Crazy?

Read each of the measurements below. Decide whether each one seems possible or crazy. Circle your answer. Use an inch ruler to help you decide.

1. A big toe is 5 inches long.

    could be   crazy

2. My teacher's foot is 10 inches long.

    could be   crazy

3. The length of a pencil is 20 inches.

    could be   crazy

4. The height of Bessie's doll is 25 inches.

    could be   crazy

5. Name something that could be 50 inches long.

    _____

6. Name an object for which 50 inches is a crazy measurement.

    _____

Patterns and Designs

	Student Guide	Adventure Book	Unit Resource Guide*
Lesson 1			
Line Up!	●		
Lesson 2			
Pick Apart a Pattern	●		
Lesson 3			
Name Patterns	●		
Lesson 4			
Pattern Block Symmetry	●		
Lesson 5			
Balancing Act	●		

Unit Resource Guide pages are from the teacher materials.

Name _____ Date _____

Translating and Recording Patterns

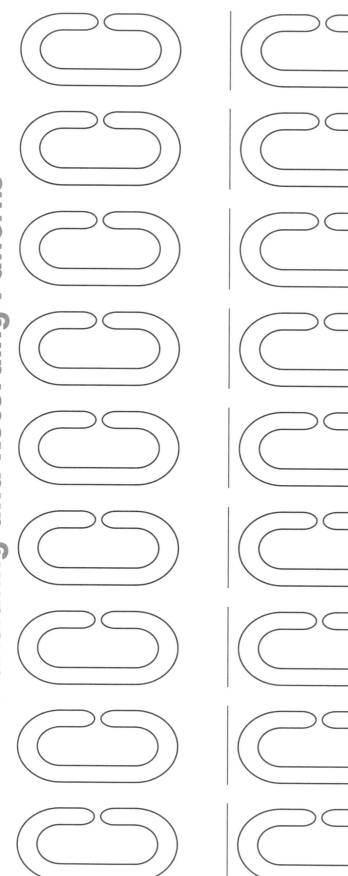

Name _____   Date _____

Colors and Shapes

What patterns do you see?

Colors:

1.

2.

3.

Shapes:

4.

5.

6.

7.

8.

Dinosaurs, Diamonds, and Dog Biscuits

What patterns do you see?

1.

2.

3.

4.

5.

6.

7.

8.

Pick Apart a Pattern

Super Sleuth

Record the pattern shown on the lines below.

1.

_____

2.

_____

3.

_____

4.

_____

Twins

Write A, B, or C on the line under each object to show the pattern. Draw a ring around the repeating pattern unit.

1.

_____

2.

_____

3.

_____

4.

_____

Name Grid

Use your first name to create a name grid pattern. Write one letter of your name in each box. Color the last letter of your name each time it occurs. Be careful not to skip any boxes.

Ten-by-Ten Name Grid

Homework

Dear Family Member:

Help your child create a name grid pattern. He or she should fill the grid by writing his or her first name many times in the boxes. One letter should go in each box. Then, have your child color the last letter of his or her name each time it occurs. Here is an example of a smaller name grid pattern for Kim:

Thank you for your help.

K	I	M	K
I	M	K	I
M	K	I	M
K	I	M	K

Write your first name in the boxes below. Put one letter in each box.

Names and Grids

The last letter of the name will be in a shaded box.

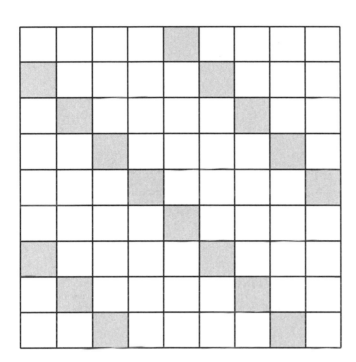

1. Circle the name that fits the pattern on this grid.

   Maggie

   Lynne

   Van

   Miko

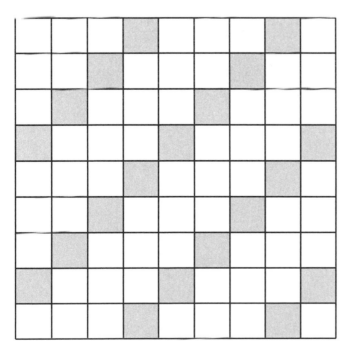

2. Write a name that fits the pattern on this grid.

   _____

Name _____   Date _____

Trapezoid Man

1. Cover this side.   **2.** Make this side balance.

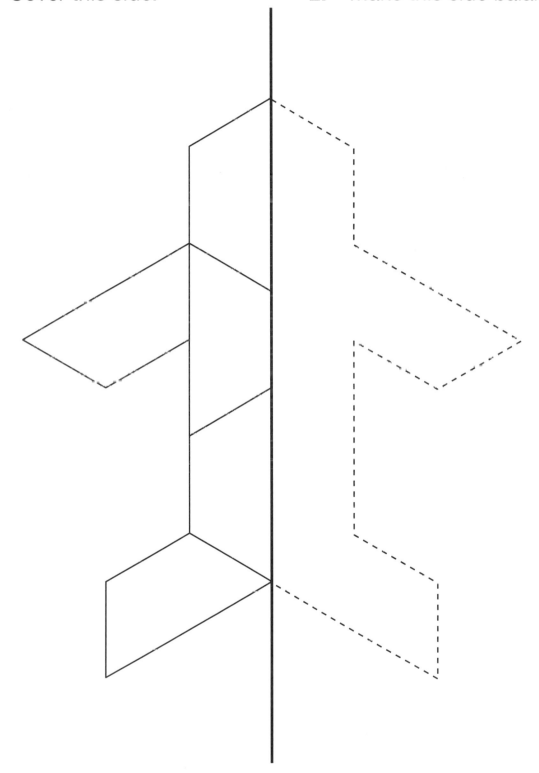

Butterfly

1. Cover this side.

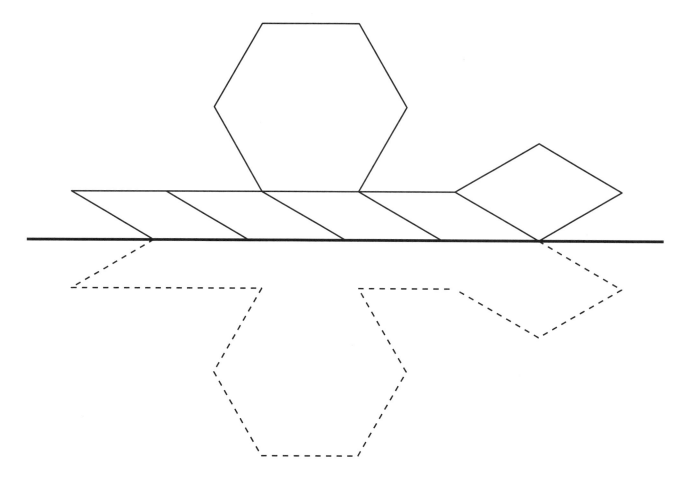

2. Make this side balance.

Van's Coin Jar

Dear Family Member:

Use a small jar of coins that contains nickels, dimes, and pennies.

Thank you.

Follow these steps:

1. **Pull a few coins from the jar.**

2. **Find the value of the coins.**

3. **Record the amount on the data table in the My Coins column.**

4. **Repeat two more times.**

Data Table

Pull	Van's Coins	My Coins
1	27¢	
2	34¢	
3	19¢	

Who pulled more money for each pull, Van or you? Circle the amount that shows more money.

Name _____   Date _____

Tree

1. Cover this side.   **2.** Make this side balance.

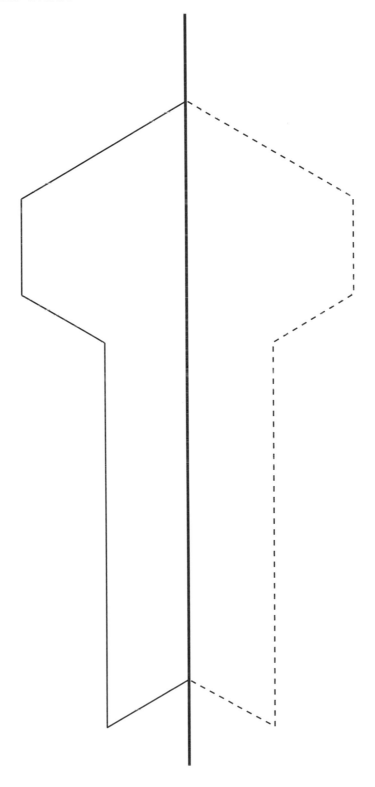

Balancing Act

Use pattern blocks to make a balanced design.

Subtracting to Solve Problems

	Student Guide	Adventure Book	Unit Resource Guide*
Lesson 1			
At the Circus			
Lesson 2			
Our Own Stories	●		
Lesson 3			
Clowning Around	●		●
Lesson 4			
How Many in the Bag?	●		
Lesson 5			
Making Flip Books			●

*Unit Resource Guide pages are from the teacher materials.

Whole-Part-Part Mat

Whole

Part

Part

Recording Subtraction Sentences

_____ – _____ = _____ whole part part	_____ – _____ = _____ whole part part
_____ – _____ = _____ whole part part	_____ – _____ = _____ whole part part
_____ – _____ = _____ whole part part	_____ – _____ = _____ whole part part
_____ – _____ = _____ whole part part	_____ – _____ = _____ whole part part

Subtraction Story

Dear Family Member:

At school, we are working on subtraction problems by drawing pictures of take-away stories. Ask your child to tell a take-away story. Write down your child's story as he or she tells it to you. Your child should then illustrate the story and write a number sentence for it.

Thank you for your cooperation.

_____ − _____ = _____
     whole   *part*   *part*

Name _____ Date _____

Taking Home Subtraction Cartoons

Dear Family Member:

Your child illustrated a subtraction story in class. Encourage your child to illustrate another subtraction story based on a subtraction number sentence. Help your child choose an appropriate number sentence such as $9 - 4 = 5$ or $12 - 3 = 9$. Ask your child to read the subtraction sentence and tell the story that he or she illustrates. You can help your child by asking him or her to identify the whole, the part that is taken away, and the part that is left.

Please send the subtraction cartoon story to school tomorrow so that your child can share it with the class.

Thank you for your help.

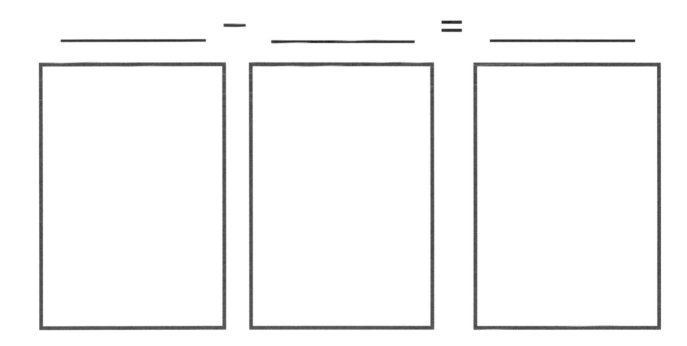

Name _____ Date _____

How Many in the Bag?

_____ – _____ = _____
in the bag   taken out   left in the bag

_____ – _____ = _____
in the bag   taken out   left in the bag

_____ – _____ = _____
in the bag   taken out   left in the bag

_____ – _____ = _____
in the bag   taken out   left in the bag

_____ – _____ = _____
in the bag   taken out   left in the bag

_____ – _____ = _____
in the bag   taken out   left in the bag

_____ – _____ = _____
in the bag   taken out   left in the bag

_____ – _____ = _____
in the bag   taken out   left in the bag

Counting Up at Home

🎒 Homework

Dear Family Member:

In class, your child has been playing *How Many in the Bag?* with a partner. We would like you to play this game with your child. To play, you will need a bag and 20 beans (or other objects).

1. Put between 10 and 20 beans in a bag. Write the number of objects on the bag.

2. Pull out at least half of the beans, and place them on the table. Ask your child to count them.

3. Without looking in the bag, your child should figure out how many beans are left in the bag.

4. He or she should record the number sentence for this problem on the lines provided below and on the following page.

5. Repeat this activity until the lines are filled.

Ask your child how he or she found the answer. Children use many strategies for solving problems. One strategy often used by young children is called counting up. For example, if there are 14 beans in the bag and 11 are taken out, the child might count from 11 to 14 to find how many are left in the bag: "12, 13, 14." Since three more were counted, three is the answer.

Thank you.

_____ – _____ = _____
in the bag   *taken out*   *left in the bag*

_____ – _____ = _____
in the bag   *taken out*   *left in the bag*

_____ – _____ = _____
in the bag   *taken out*   *left in the bag*

_____ – _____ = _____
in the bag   *taken out*   *left in the bag*

_____ – _____ = _____
in the bag   *taken out*   *left in the bag*

_____ – _____ = _____
in the bag   *taken out*   *left in the bag*

_____ – _____ = _____
in the bag   *taken out*   *left in the bag*

_____ – _____ = _____
in the bag   *taken out*   *left in the bag*

Grouping by Tens

	Student Guide	Adventure Book	Unit Resource Guide*
Lesson 1			
Spill the Beans	●		
Lesson 2			
More or Less than 100?	●		
Lesson 3			
Spin for Beans	●		●
Lesson 4			
The 50 Chart	●		●
Lesson 5			
The 100 Chart	●		●
Lesson 6			
Measuring with Connecting Links	●		
Lesson 7			
Numbers in the News	●		●
Lesson 8			
Full of Beans	●		

Unit Resource Guide pages are from the teacher materials.

Group and Count

Dear Family Member:

In class, we are counting by grouping objects in tens and leftover ones. You can help provide additional practice for your child by gathering a collection of objects and setting it out for your child to group and count. Change the total number of objects at least two times. Some ideas for objects to use are cereal pieces, nuts, pasta, raisins, pennies, buttons, and marbles. There should be 40–70 objects each time your child groups and counts.

Thank you for your cooperation.

Find objects to count. Ask an adult or an older sister or brother to help you.

Object	Number of Groups of 10	Number of Leftovers	Number

Return this paper on _____.

Name _____ Date _____

How Many Letters?

Write the first names of four people or pets at home. Write the number of letters in each name.

First Name	Number of Letters

Total Number of Letters = _____

Draw a picture or tell how you found the total number of letters.

Return this sheet to school by _____.

Spin for Beans 50

Players

This is a game for two or more players.

Materials

- *Spin for Beans 50 Playing Mat*
- *Spin for Beans 50 Recording Sheet*
- 50 baby lima beans for each player
- clear plastic spinner or a pencil and paper clip

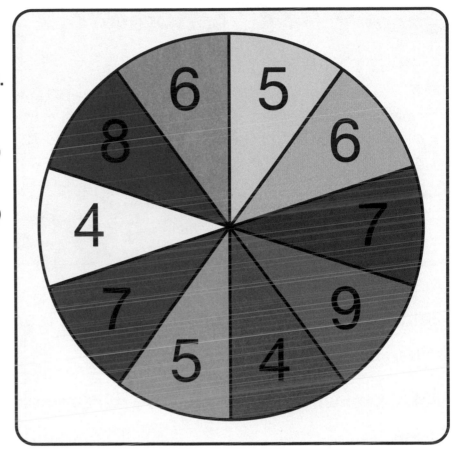

Rules

1. Place a plastic spinner over the spinner above. If you do not have a clear spinner, use a pencil and a paper clip.

2. Spin to find out how many beans to take.

3. Place the beans on the ten frame on the playing mat. Put one bean in each square.

4. Write the number of tens you have collected so far. Use your recording sheet. Write the number of leftover ones you have too.

5. Write the total number of beans you have.

6. Each time you spin, add the beans to your collection on the ten frames until someone collects 50 beans.

Spin for Beans at Home

Homework

Make a tally mark for each person you teach to play the game.

Tallies _____

Make a tally mark for every five minutes you play the game.

Tallies _____   Total Minutes _____

Parent's Signature _____

Child's Signature _____

Return this sheet to school by _____.

Name _____ Date _____

50 Chart

<table>
<tr><td></td><td></td><td></td><td></td><td></td></tr>
<tr><td></td><td></td><td></td><td></td><td></td></tr>
<tr><td></td><td></td><td></td><td></td><td></td></tr>
<tr><td></td><td></td><td></td><td></td><td></td></tr>
<tr><td></td><td></td><td></td><td></td><td></td></tr>
<tr><td></td><td></td><td></td><td></td><td></td></tr>
<tr><td></td><td></td><td></td><td></td><td></td></tr>
<tr><td></td><td></td><td></td><td></td><td></td></tr>
<tr><td></td><td></td><td></td><td></td><td></td></tr>
<tr><td></td><td></td><td></td><td></td><td></td></tr>
</table>

Name _____ Date _____

100 Chart

1	2	3	4	5	6	7	8	9	10
11	12	13	14	15	16	17	18	19	20
21	22	23	24	25	26	27	28	29	30
31	32	33	34	35	36	37	38	39	40
41	42	43	44	45	46	47	48	49	50
51	52	53	54	55	56	57	58	59	60
61	62	63	64	65	66	67	68	69	70
71	72	73	74	75	76	77	78	79	80
81	82	83	84	85	86	87	88	89	90
91	92	93	94	95	96	97	98	99	100

Counting by Tens

Count by tens. Fill in the missing numbers. Then, color the *100 Chart*.

yellow	green	orange	blue	red	purple
8	10	2			
18					
28			25		
38					36
				51	

Guess My Number

Dear Family Member:

Your child is learning about locating and placing numbers in intervals. Help your child locate numbers in intervals by playing *Guess My Number.* Your child has practiced this game in class. The rules are listed below. We recommend that you use numbers that are between 1 and 20 to start.

Thank you.

Players

This is a game for two or more players.

Materials

Players can use a calendar, a *100 Chart,* or a centimeter ruler to help find the number.

Rules

1. Player 1: Selects a number.

   For example, "I am thinking of a number that is between _____ and _____."

2. Player 2: Tries to guess the number Player 1 has selected.

3. Player 1: Corrects Player 2's guess by saying either "It is lower" or "It is higher."

4. Player 2: Continues to make guesses as Player 1 continues to give out clues.

Play ends when Player 2 guesses the number.

Find Numbers in the News

Homework

Dear Family Member:

Help your child find a newspaper headline with a number in it. Glue the headline in the space provided on the back of this paper. If your child cannot find one in the newspaper, circle one of the headlines below.

To get your child started, write one sentence that compares the number to other numbers. For example, 34 is 10 more than 24. More examples are listed for the number 34 below.

Encourage your child to think of his or her own sentences. He or she should record them on the lines provided on the back of this paper.

Thank you for your cooperation.

13-Hour Sale

32 TOTAL BODY EXERCISES

Dist. 87 gets tougher on bad checks

60 years later, medals honor veterans of World War II

34 Kids Think in Math Marathon

34 is
- large compared to 5;
- about the same size as 30;
- a lot less than 100;
- between 30 and 40;
- 10 more than 24;
- 10 less than 44;
- 1 more than 33;
- 1 less than 35.

Name _____ Date _____

Paste your headline below.

_____

_____

_____

_____

_____

_____

_____

_____

Full of Beans

Draw

Draw a picture of the lab setup.

Fill in the data tables.

Group Data Table

Kind of Bean	Number of Beans

Class Data Table

Kind of Bean	Number of Beans

Name _____ Date _____

Full of Beans Class Data

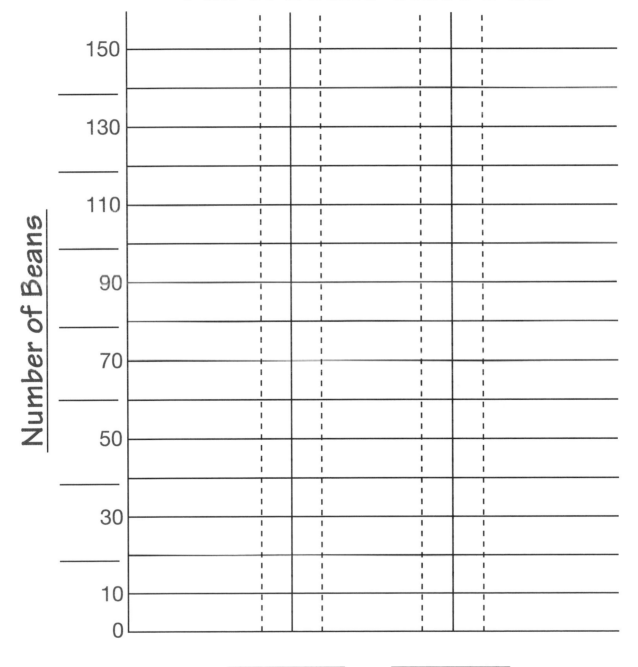

Explore

1. Which kind of bean did your cup hold more of?

   _____

   About how many more? Use your graph to help you.

   _____

2. Which kind of bean was bigger in size?

   _____

3. Will a cup always hold more small beans than big beans? Explain your answer.

   _____

   _____

   _____

4. Work with your partner to answer this question. Then, share with the class how you found your answer.

   If we had a big cup that holds 200 of the small beans, about how many large beans would the cup hold?

   _____

Full of Beans

Name _____   Date _____

Maria and José's Graph

Maria and José did the *Full of Beans* experiment with lima beans and kidney beans. Here is a bar graph of their data.

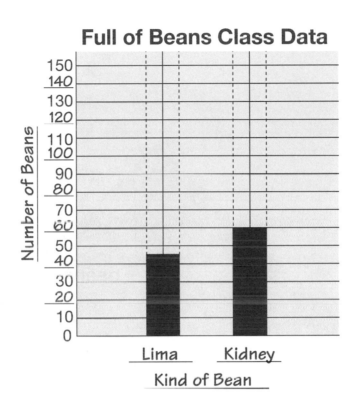

1. About how many lima beans were in the cup? _____

2. Which bean was bigger in size, the lima bean or the kidney bean?

   _____

3. About how many more kidney beans were there than lima beans?

   _____

Measurement: Area

	Student Guide	Adventure Book	Unit Resource Guide*
Lesson 1			
Finding Area with Pennies	●		
Lesson 2			
Goldilocks and the Three Rectangles	●		
Lesson 3			
How Much Area?	●		
Lesson 4			
The Midnight Visit		●	
Lesson 5			
Unit Designs	●		

Unit Resource Guide pages are from the teacher materials.

Partly Cloudy

Name _____ Date _____

More Clouds

Cloud A

How many pennies? _____

Cloud B

How many pennies? _____

Draw a Shape

Dear Family Member:

In class your child measured the area of shapes by counting the number of pennies needed to cover each shape. Please gather pennies and quarters for your child so he or she may have more practice finding area. Help your child complete the questions below. Thank you for your help.

Draw a large shape in the space below. Then, answer the questions.

1. Cover the shape with pennies. How many cover the shape?

   _____

2. Cover the shape with quarters. How many cover the shape?

   _____

3. Did more pennies or more quarters fit in the shape? Explain why you think more of this coin fit in the shape.

   _____

Goldilocks and the Three Rectangles

The Three Rectangles

Randy
Rectangle

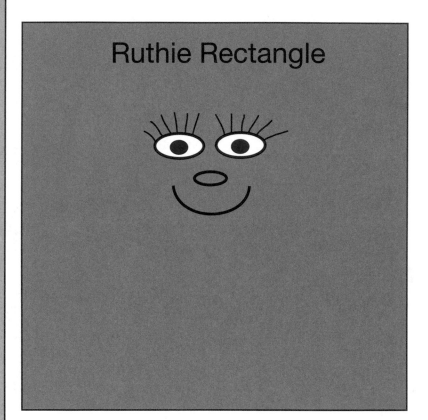

Ruthie Rectangle

Rebecca Rectangle

Goldilocks and the Three Rectangles

Rectangle Table

Record the measurements in the table below.

Name	Tall (in inches)	Wide (in inches)	Area (in square inches)
Randy			
Rebecca			
Ruthie			

Name _____   Date _____

Rupert Rectangle

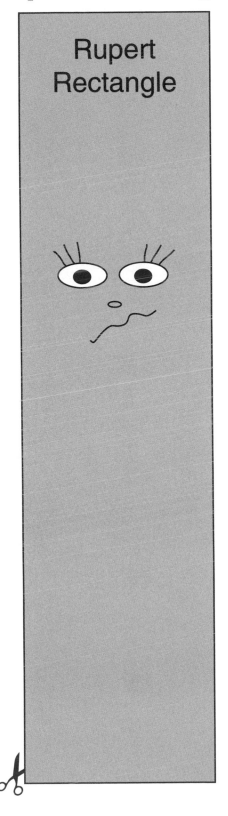

Rupert
Rectangle

Square Inches

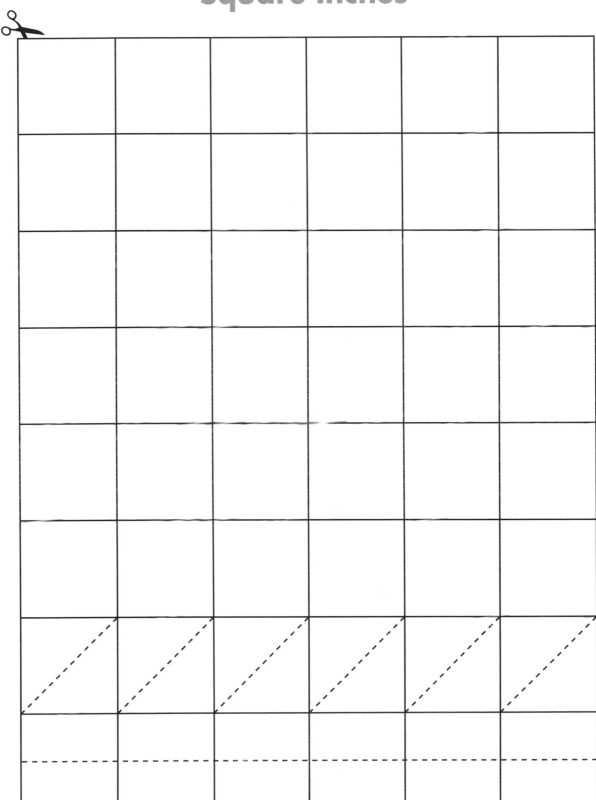

Tiles 1

Find the area of each figure. Use square-inch tiles and halves of square-inch tiles.

1. _____ square inches   **2.** _____ square inches

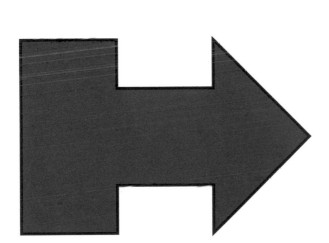 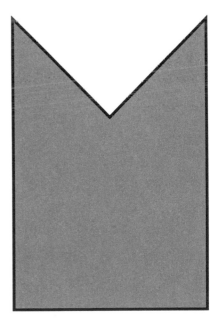

3. _____ square inches   **4.** _____ square inches

Tiles 2

Find the area of each figure. Use square-inch tiles and halves of square-inch tiles.

1. _____
square
inches

2. _____
square
inches

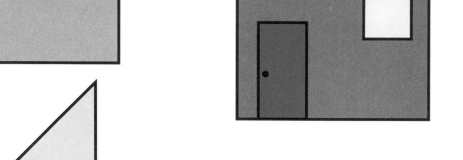

3. _____
square
inches

4. _____
square
inches

Tiles 3

**What is the area of each shape?
Use square-inch tiles and halves
of square-inch tiles to help you.**

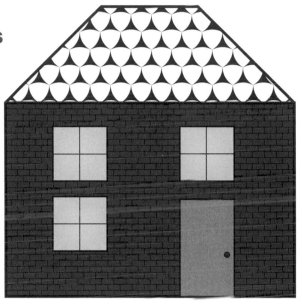

1. _____ square inches

2. _____ square inches   **3.** _____ square inches

Unit Designs

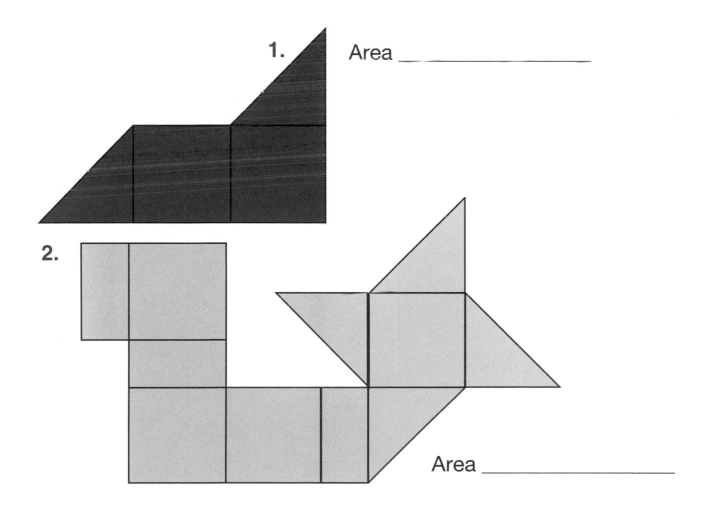

Homework

Dear Family Member:

In class your child created a design similar to those below using square-inch and half-square-inch pieces. To find the area of the shapes, your child will count full square inches and piece half-square inches together to make more wholes. Check that your child records the area for each shape and includes the unit of measure, "square inches." Thank you.

Find the area of each of the shapes. Include in your answer the number and unit.

1.   Area _____

2.   Area _____

Name _____ Date _____

3.

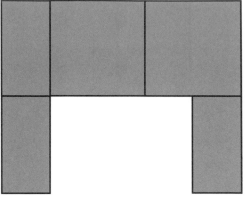

Area _____

4.

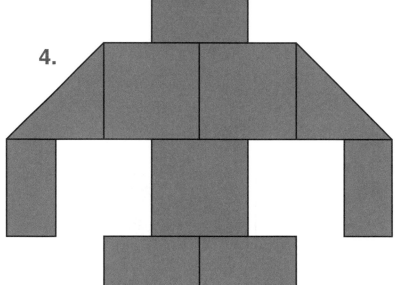

Area _____

Unit Designs

Which Two?

Find the area of each shape. Use your tiles. There is one shape on the next page.

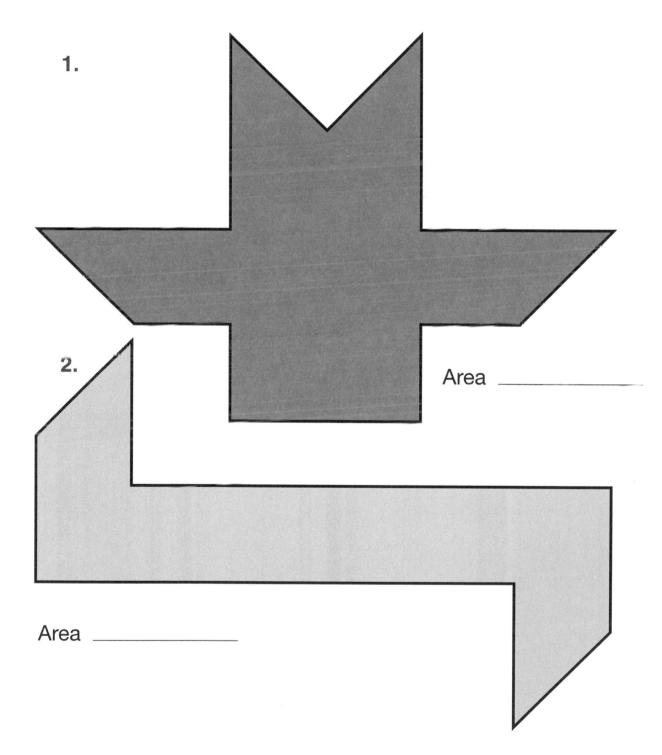

1.

Area _____

2.

Area _____

3.

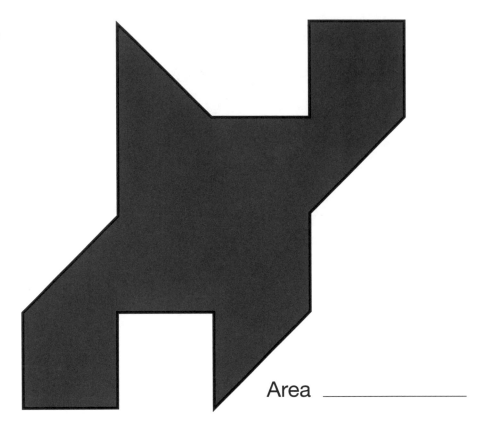

Area _____

4. Which two shapes have the same area?

_____

5. Does the other shape have a larger or smaller area?

_____

Glossary

This glossary provides definitions or examples of key terms in the Grade 1 lessons as a resource for students and parents. See the Glossary in the *Teacher Implementation Guide* for more precise definitions.

A

Area (Unit 10)
The amount of space that a shape covers. Area is measured in square units.

B

C

Circumference (Unit 15)
The distance around a circle.

Counting All (Unit 1)
A strategy for counting and adding in which students start at one and count until the total is reached.

Counting On (Unit 1, Unit 4)
A strategy for counting or adding objects in which students start from a larger number and then count until the total is reached. For example, to count 6 + 3, begin with 6 and count three more, 7, 8, 9.

Cube (Unit 12, Unit 15)
A three-dimensional shape with six square faces that are all the same size.

Cubic Unit (Unit 12)
A unit for measuring volume—a cube that measures one unit along each edge. For example, cubic centimeters and cubic inches are standard units of measure.

cubic centimeter

Cylinder (Unit 15)
A three-dimensional shape. Examples:

Cylinders   Not a Cylinder

D

Data Table
A tool for recording and organizing information.

Name	Age

E

Edge (Unit 15)
A line segment where two faces of a three-dimensional figure meet.

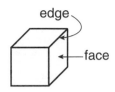

Estimate (Unit 12)
1. To find *about* how many (as a verb).
2. An approximate number (as a noun).

Even Number (Unit 4)
Numbers that are doubles. The numbers 0, 2, 4, 6, 8, 10, . . . etc. are even. The number 28 is even because it is 14 + 14.

F

Face (Unit 12)
A two-dimensional shape that is one side of a three-dimensional shape.

Fixed Variables (Unit 2, Unit 11)
Variables in an experiment that do not change.

G

H

Hexagon (Unit 2)
A six-sided polygon.

Hexagons   Not Hexagons

I

J

K

L

Length
The distance along a line or curve from one point to another. Distance can be measured with a ruler or tape measure. Distance can also be measured in paces, handspans, and other nonstandard units.

Line
A set of points that form a straight path extending infinitely in two directions.

Line Symmetry (Unit 7, Unit 18)
A shape has line symmetry if it can be folded into two matching halves.

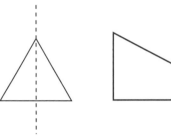

This shape has   This shape does not
line symmetry.   have line symmetry.

Line of Symmetry (Unit 7)
A line such that if a figure is folded along the line, then one half of the figure matches the other.

M

Making a Ten (Unit 13)
A strategy for adding and subtracting that takes advantage of students' knowledge of partitions of ten. For example, a student might find 8 + 4 by breaking the 4 into 2 + 2 and then using a knowledge of sums that add to ten.

$$8 + 4 =$$
$$8 + 2 + 2 =$$
$$10 + 2 = 12$$

Median (Unit 6, Unit 9)
The number "in the middle" of a set of data. Example 1: Jonah rolled a car down a ramp three times. The first time it rolled 30 cm. The second time it rolled 28 cm. The third time it rolled 33 cm. He put the numbers in order: 28 cm, 30 cm, 33 cm. The median is 30 cm because it is in the "middle" of his data. Example 2: The median of 28 cm, 30 cm, 32 cm, and 35 cm is 31 cm.

Mr. Origin (Unit 6, Unit 9)
A plastic figure used to help children learn about direction and distance.

N

Near Double (Unit 13)
A derived addition or subtraction fact found by using doubles. For example, 3 + 4 = 7 follows from the fact that 3 + 3 = 6.

Number Sentence (Unit 3)
A number sentence uses numbers and symbols instead of words to describe a problem. For example, a number sentence for the problem "Five birds landed on a branch. Then two more birds landed on the branch. How many birds are on the branch?" is 5 + 2 = 7.

O

Odd Number (Unit 4)
A number that is not even. The odd numbers are 1, 3, 5, 7, 9, and so on.

Origin (Unit 6, Unit 9)
A reference point for a coordinate system. If the coordinate system is a line, we can determine the location of an object on the line by the number of units it is to the right or the left of the origin.

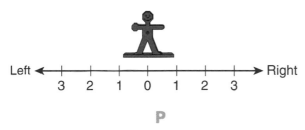

P

Pattern Unit (Unit 7)
The portion of a pattern that is repeated. For example, AAB is the pattern unit in the pattern AABAABAAB.

Perimeter (Unit 6)
The distance around a two-dimensional shape.

Polygon
A 2-dimensional shape. A closed, connected plane figure consisting of line segments, with exactly two segments meeting at each end point.

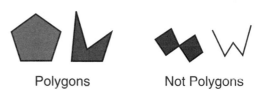

Polygons   Not Polygons

Prediction (Unit 5)
Using a sample to tell about what is likely to occur in a population.

Prism (Unit 15)
A three-dimensional shape. Examples:

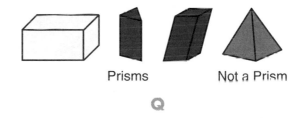

Prisms   Not a Prism

Q

Quadrilateral
A polygon with four sides.

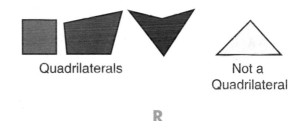

Quadrilaterals   Not a Quadrilateral

R

Rectangle (Unit 2)
A polygon with four sides and with four square corners.

Rectangles   Not a Rectangle

Rhombus (Unit 2)
A polygon with four sides of equal length.

Rhombuses   Not a Rhombus

S

Sample (Unit 5)
A smaller group taken out of a large collection.

Sphere (Unit 15)
A three-dimensional shape. A basketball is a common object shaped like a sphere.

Square (Unit 2)
A rectangle with four equal sides.

Squares   Not Squares

Symmetry (Unit 7, Unit 18)
See Line Symmetry

T

Three-dimensional Shape (Unit 15)
A figure in space that has length, width, and height.

TIMS Laboratory Method
A method that students use to organize experiments and investigations. It involves four components: draw, collect, graph, and explore. It is a way to help students learn about the scientific method. TIMS is an acronym for Teaching Integrated Mathematics and Science.

Trapezoid (Unit 2)
A shape with four sides with exactly one pair of parallel sides.

Trapezoids   Not Trapezoids

Trial (Unit 6)
One attempt in an experiment.

Triangle (Unit 2)
A polygon with three sides.

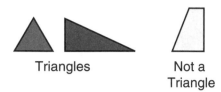

Triangles   Not a Triangle

U

Using Doubles (Unit 13)
A strategy for adding and subtracting that uses facts derived from known doubles. For example, students use $7 + 7 = 14$ to find that $7 + 8$ is one more, or 15.

Using Ten (Unit 13)
A strategy for adding and subtracting which uses reasoning from known facts. For example, students use $3 + 7 = 10$ to find that $4 + 7$ is one more, or 11.

V

Variable (Unit 2, Unit 11)
Something that changes or varies in an experiment.

Volume (Unit 9, Unit 12)
1. The amount of space an object takes up.
2. The amount of space inside a container (also called capacity).

W

X

Y

Z

Index

The index provides page references for the *Student Guide*. Definition or explanation of key terms can be found in the glossary. A good source for information on the location of topics in the curriculum is the *Scope and Sequence* in Section 5 of the *Teacher Implementation Guide*.

P

Partitioning
    numbers, 47–63, 75, 148, 404
    fifty, 213
    one hundred, 204–212
Part-part-whole problems, 49–63, 75, 148–153, 404
Patterns
    in colors and shapes, 127–131
    name grid, 133–137
    pattern blocks and, 20–23, 145
    problem solving with, 406, 411
    repeating, 126–131, 406
    translating/recording, 126
Perimeter, 100
Pictures, *See* Labs
Pets Lab, 295–299
Pocket Parts Lab, 47–53
Prediction, 97, 119–121. *See also* Labs
Prisms (boxes), 313, 319, 321, 323–324
Problem posing, 65, 296, 330
Problem solving, 65, 72–74, 237–238, 279–289,
       308–311, 328–330, 403–415. *See also* Labs,
       Word Problems
    with addition, 72–74, 279–281, 285, 289, 308–311
    with area, 410
    with coins, 65, 141, 205–211
    with multiplication, 303–305
    with subtraction, 151–153, 279–281, 285, 289,
       308–311, 328–330, 405
    with volume, 412–413
    using weather, 237–238

Q

Quarters (coins), 212–213

R

Rectangles, 13–15, 187–191, 359–366, 379–381
    in fraction puzzles, 379–381
Rhombus, 20–23
Rolling Along with Links Lab, 103–109

S

Samples, 94–97
Shapes, *See also* Line symmetry
    comparing/contrasting, 15–17, 313
    covering/construction, 19–23
    cubes, 313, 319–324
       identifying, 321–323
    cylinders (tubes), 313, 315–319, 321, 323–324
    halves of, 359–362, 367–371, 383–385
    hexagons, 15, 19–23
    identifying, 12–13, 321–325
    with pattern blocks, 19–23
    patterns with, 127–131
    prisms (boxes), 313, 319, 321, 323–324
    properties, 15–17, 313, 317–318
    rectangles, 13–15, 187–191, 359–366, 379–381
    squares, 13, 20–23
    three-dimensional, 246–261, 313–326. *See also*
       cubes, cylinders (tubes), prisms (boxes),
       spheres (balls)
    trapezoids, 20–23
    triangles, 13, 17, 19–23
    two-dimensional, 12–23
Skip counting
    by tens, 87, 90–91, 167–169, 349–351
    by twos, 84–85
Sorting, 333–334
Spheres (balls), 313, 321–325
Spin for Beans 50 Game, 163–165
Square inch tiles, 193–202
Squares, 13, 20–23
    and fractions, 359–365, 371–373, 379–381
Subtraction, 148–153, 404. *See also* Word Problems,
       Part-Part-Whole Problems
    counting up/back, 157
    halving numbers as, 277
    number sentences, 149–158, 205–206, 209–210
    problem solving with, 151–153, 279–281, 285, 289,
       308–311, 328–330, 405
Survey, 331, 337
Symmetry, *See* Line symmetry

Tallying, 27, 32–33, 164, 242–243, 337, 343
Ten Frames, 35–43, 87
    empty, 35, 43
    in identifying numbers, 37
Tens
    counting by, 87, 90–91, 167–169, 264, 279–281,
        348–351
    grouping by, 160, 163–165, 348 351
Think and Spin Game, 41
TIMS Laboratory Investigations, *See* Labs
Trapezoid, 20–23
Triangles, 13, 17, 19–23
    and fractions, 359, 362, 371

U.S. Department of Agriculture, 338
Units, *See* Length, Area, and Volume
USA map, 241

Weather, 25–29, 227–239
    calendar for recording, 25–29, 227
    comparing, 239–241
    problem solving using, 237–238
Weather 1: Eye on the Sky Lab, 25–29
Weather 2: Winter Skies Lab, 229–239
What's in That Pocket? Lab, 55–63
Whole-Part-Part mat, 148
Word problems, 279–281, 285, 289, 293–294,
        299–305, 328–329, 405, 406, 409, 412,
        413, 414. *See also* Labs

Volume, 246–261
    comparing, 247, 249, 255, 261
    cube models and, 246–249
    of cubic animals, 259–261
    estimating, 247–249
    problem solving with, 412 413